The Stori Book of Embellishing

Great Ideas for Quilts and Garments

BY MARY STORI

American Quilter's Society

P.O. Box 3290

Paducah, KY 42002-3290

Library of Congress Cataloging-in-Publication Data

Stori, Mary.
The Stori book of embellishing: great ideas for quilts or garments/by Mary Stori.
p.   cm.
ISBN 0-89145-843-3: $16.95
1. Appliqué. 2. Patchwork. 3. Wearable art. I. Title
TT779.S69 1994   94-22377
746.44′5--dc20   CIP

Additional copies of this book may be ordered from:

American Quilter's Society
P.O. Box 3290
Paducah, KY 42002-3290

@$16.95. Add $1.00 for postage & handling.

■ Dedication ■

To DAVID
FOR NURTURING MY POTENTIAL

■ Acknowledgments ■

A special thank you to the following for their friendship, support, and encouragement: Betty Micheels, Chris DeTomasi, Shirley Fomby, Francie Ginocchio, Doreen Speckmann, and Carol Doak. I'm grateful to all the folks at American Quilter's Society, especially my editor, Victoria Faoro. My appreciation is also extended to Pfaff American Sales Corporation and Sulky of America for their generosity.

Table of Contents

RIGHT, TOP: **AND SO THEY WERE MOORRIED**, vest, front view, 1994. (Detail, page 36.)
PHOTO: JIM ALEXANDER NEWBERRY

RIGHT, BOTTOM: **AND SO THEY WERE MOORRIED**, vest, back view, 1994. (Detail, page 36.)
PHOTO: JIM ALEXANDER NEWBERRY

Introduction

Most professional stitchers I know can remember using a needle and thread at age five. They speak proudly of watching their mothers and grandmothers sew. Others can recite a list of impressive degrees and credentials earned in the field of fiber arts. Since none of the above apply to me, I was tempted to avoid my background! There were no quiltmakers in my family. In fact, with the exception of making minor repairs, our sewing machine was rarely used. Oh, I had the humbling experience of making a gathered skirt in junior high school and remember being frustrated and embarrassed over the entire effort! The fact is, I didn't become a sewer until well after I'd embarked on another satisfying career.

As a cookbook author and cooking instructor, my time was spent happily slicing and dicing, until a series of back operations demanded a lifestyle change. There I was, stuck in a cast from my pelvis to my neck, considering that just possibly, it was time for the ultimate, grand sulk! Enter, Mother-in-law to the rescue. One look at my pouting face convinced her I needed a project.

She wasn't a quiltmaker, but had always sewn. She'd recently begun incorporating some patchwork in her clothing projects, a direct influence of a wearable art class she'd attended. Her enthusiasm for patchwork, along with my country decorating style, led to the suggestion of making patchwork pillows for my family room.

Everyone has a beginning and that was mine. But how on earth did I make the leap from non-sewer to fiber artist? Those patchwork pillows led to quiltmaking and eventually I was bitten by the wearable art bug! I soon recognized that my new interest was outweighed by my lack of know-how. I've always maintained that my biggest hindrance is my lack of formal training, and my biggest asset is my lack of formal training. If you don't know the rules, it's easy to break them!

As I began to experiment with my own ideas, it became necessary to develop methods I could execute to accomplish a particular task. It was easier for me to add a button or bead, rather than appliqué a circle. My interest in embellishments started out as a means to an end...or should I say short-cut. Certainly, I could have taken the time to learn to properly appliqué a circle, but I was too impatient! After becoming smitten with the uniqueness of wearables, I eagerly attempted to create my own. Without the benefit of a solid background in construction methods, it was often a struggle. Of course, I avoided garments that were complicated and difficult to sew because I didn't have a clue how to make them! Instead, I selected simple patterns. The trouble was they looked **simple** and were **boring**. The solution for me was easy; rather then sewing the design into the garment, I added it on. Adding embellishments was definitely the right answer for me, since it made an ordinary project unique. The embellishments became the design, and at other times served to enhance designs already in place.

This book explores embellishments suitable for quilts and garments. It contains innovative approaches to challenge the advanced sewer, and allows the beginner to progress as her experience grows. Rather than providing patterns for you to duplicate, the goal is to present imaginative and creative ideas to be used as a reference for your own projects. It is not intended to teach you to make quilts or construct garments. A certain level of experience is taken for granted. Stores and libraries (and perhaps your own personal sewing library) are full of books that furnish precise instructions for these fundamentals. They include excellent general information regarding fabrics, battings, and equipment most often used.

The primary aim of course is to offer ideas, options, and advice which will supply the necessary knowledge for you to create projects that incorporate embellishments. By presenting what is possible, it's my hope that inspiration will follow. Above all enjoy yourself, but remember, embellishing can be addictive and time consuming. Consider surrendering without a fight! You'll then be free to explore its possibilities and opportunities.

Chapter One

ABOVE: QUEEN OF HEARTS, front view,
1992. (Back view, page 57; details 9, 69).

PHOTO: RICHARD WALKER

ABOVE: **QUEEN OF HEARTS**, detail. (Front view, page 8, back view, page 57; detail, page 69.)
PHOTO: RICHARD WALKER

The First Step

- ■ Embellishments & Their Role
- ■ Designing with Embellishments
- ■ Suggested Embellishments

THE FIRST STEP

What began as a simple flirtation with a few buttons and beads has become a love affair. Now, most of my work incorporates multiple embellishment methods. The initial idea for this book was to present various methods of surface design so readers could apply similar approaches to their work. Through experience I've learned that to achieve a harmonious finished piece, the fabric construction and embellishment techniques must be compatible. In order to equip you with the best opportunity for success, I concluded that the information needed to be treated as a complete package. It is my overall approach to embellishing that I hope to share. In theory, it would seem possible to add any type of embellishment to any type of project at any stage of the construction...but

that just isn't the case. You'd be terribly frustrated if you spent a month beading a jacket, only to realize that through the process the material had "shrunk," resulting in a garment that doesn't fit! By comprehending the big picture you will avoid those disappointments!

Perhaps your immediate goal is to add a few beads to a completed project or determine what embellishments to use on a project. By exploring the ideas offered in the last chapter, Embellishing Methods, you'll become sufficiently educated to make informed choices. Some may be familiar; you've seen beading and embroidery on crazy quilts and various fabric manipulations on lovely Baltimore Album quilts. My style developed as I incorporated standard techniques, which eventually led to my discovering new ones.

■ Embellishments and Their Role ■

Okay, so what is the meaning of the term "embellishments"? In the simplest form it can be defined as decoration or adornment. To embellish is to adorn, bedeck, decorate, enhance, dress up, beautify, and glamorize. Let's think about those words. Have you ever watched the Academy Awards? If your answer is yes, I'll bet you've noticed plenty of beaded and sequined gowns. Country music stars use the glitz and glitter of rhinestones and sequins to make their costumes sparkle under the lights. These beads, rhinestones, and sequins are all forms of embellishment used to enhance the garment. Embellishments are usually ornamental and not intended to be functional. Of course, they can also serve a multi-purpose role. An unusual coin placed near the edge of the center front opening of a jacket could be considered decorative, but it may also serve as a closure. In general, embellishments are the little extras that make a project unique.

Fortunately, surface design opportunities go way beyond beads, rhinestones, and sequins. Of course, my explanation cited the flashy add-ons because these items are the first thing most of us identify with when referring to embellishments. Creative embellishing involves being able to visualize both common and uncommon articles as embellishments. The ability to utilize and incorporate a diverse inventory of items into a project is exciting. Don't let this confuse you; even very familiar techniques such as embroidery can be classified as embellishment. Conventional and distinctive embellishments can work in harmony as they have done in the quilt TAKARA. A simple embroidered stem stitch created the facial features of the lovely lady, while the unusual touch of silk flowers adorn her hair. An antique petit point obe sash was the perfect choice to duplicate the look of a fancy fan handle. Naturally, the imaginative use of the flowers and sash presented obstacles. Since this section is intended as an introduction,

I'm afraid I've teased you with this illustration. You will find the methods involved in creating the details of this project in the last chapter. (See Oddities, page 92.) At this time, I'd prefer to discuss some insights I've gained from creating my embellished artwork, to prepare you for the information in the following chapters.

My personal definition of the word "embellish" is "the icing on the cake." Now I didn't say how thick, or that it had to be chocolate! That would depend upon the type of cake and the taste of the person making it. What do cake and icing have to do with the subject of this book? They're my simple analogy to help explain that the type of surface designs and the role they play are determined by many factors.

One element that directly influences the end result is the person doing the embellishing. If the level of skill and experience is vast, you might automatically assume their potential for accomplishment is greater than that of a beginner. This is not always the case. The creative talents and personality traits that each possess can alter the outcome. A less experienced sewer with a positive "can do" attitude may be more likely to complete an ambitious project than the experienced stitcher who's lazy or is easily bored. Personal preferences also have an impact on embellishing decisions. Each of us has our own personal interpretation of what constitutes glamour. For instance, decorating a velvet jacket with a zillion sequins or rhinestones may be appealing to one, but distasteful to another.

The project to be embellished is another component that affects the selection of embellishments. Is it a garment or a quilt? Will you be adding embellishments to a previously prepared project? Are you creating a piece specifically for the items you wish to feature? Will the work be washed? Is it large or small?

My suggestions and your experience will prepare you to make informed decisions regarding the role embellishments will play in your work. Acknowledging the myriad of details that determine the appropriateness of the embellishments to the project can be time-consuming, but is very necessary.

RIGHT: **MILITARY MITE**, front view, Mary Stori, 1990.

PHOTO: RICHARD WALKER

■ Designing with Embellishments ■

In order to integrate the fabric construction, design, and embellishing process, it's valuable to understand the relationship between them. Always remember, your embellishments become a part (whether large or small) of the design. They can even **be** the design, as in the case with my jacket MILITARY MITE. This example clearly illustrates how important the partnership between embellishment design and construction can be. During a cleaning frenzy, I came upon a bunch of forgotten military decorations which my husband no longer wanted. I decided to rescue them from the inevitable trip to a landfill by using them to decorate my well-broken-in denim jacket. Realizing

that had been done before, after some pondering, I embarked upon making a corduroy jacket to feature these treasures. What seemed to be an adequate amount of "stuff" when I began, looked pretty puny at second glance. My mission for the next few months was to haunt flea markets, garage sales, and antique stores looking for additional pieces. Finally, I was satisfied with the composition and enthusiastically completed the garment. As you can observe, the sturdy fabric played a key role by providing the necessary support for all the pins and medals.

In most cases, my embellishing is completed toward the conclusion of the construction phase of the work. That generally means before a quilt is backed, or prior to sewing a garment together and adding the lining. But that doesn't mean I wait until that point to make my plans. Any time I spend in advance considering my embellishing options tends to pay off later. For instance, when sewing one of my earlier garments, I decided to add some buttons to hide an unattractive seam line. I was so anxious to complete the garment, that the next time I thought about adding these embellishing details, the entire jacket was finished. Since the lining was already in place, adding the buttons became a trick! Had I thought things through and done a little planning, the process of sewing on the buttons could have been completed in a quarter of the time and with me in much better humor!

Another purpose embellishing serves is to enhance and strengthen the design. Notice how a few well placed beads on the flowers of my jumper MARY, MARY, HOW DOES YOUR GARDEN GROW? WHY WITH FABRIC, OF COURSE! #2 (right) added some pizzazz. A further function is the combination of the two objectives.

So what is embellishing? Just what I said... the "icing on the cake." Feel free to enhance your projects with as few or as many techniques as you please. As you study examples pictured throughout the book, consider the role embellishing has played in my designs. I think you'll agree that the pieces would lose some of their personality if the details were eliminated.

RIGHT: MARY, MARY, HOW DOES YOUR GARDEN GROW? WHY WITH FABRIC, OF COURSE! #2, detail. (Front view, page 50; details, page 52, 59.)

PHOTO: RICHARD WALKER

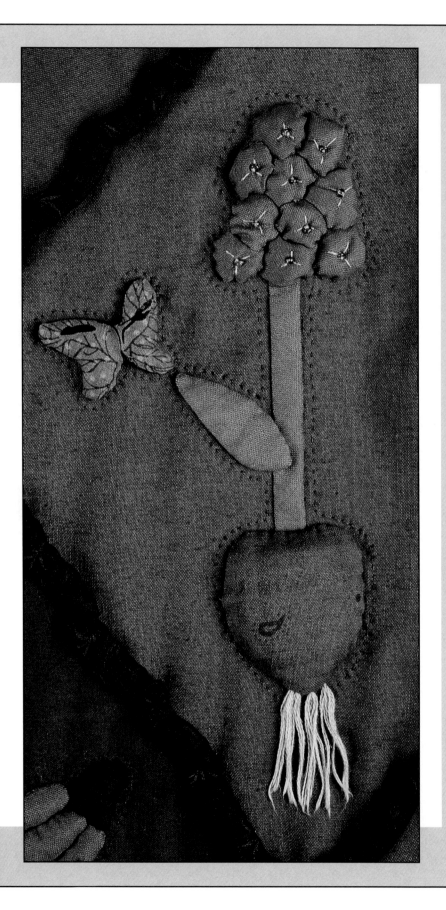

■ Suggested ■ Embellishments

This list is presented in no particular order or preference. It certainly shouldn't be considered a complete list, merely suggestions to explore. Please refer to the final chapter where methods of treating various embellishments are located.

BEADS
BUTTONS
SEQUINS
CHARMS
TRINKETS
DECORATIVE THREADS
PLASTIC
BUCKLES
PINS
COSTUME JEWELRY
PATCHES & BADGES
RIBBONS
LACE
SEASHELLS
ULTRA-SUEDE®
PHOTOCOPIES
IMAGE TRANSFER
TRIMS
CORDING
PAINTING
EMBROIDERY
MINIATURES
YARN
SEWING NOTIONS
SILK FLOWERS
SPECIALITY FABRICS –
lamés, satins, sheers, upholstery

Chapter Two

ABOVE: **SEW PUZZLED**, jacket, front view,
(skirt and blouse, page 18.)

PHOTO: JIM ALEXANDER NEWBERRY

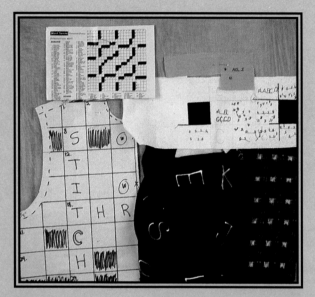

ABOVE: Newspaper clipping that inspired the vest and paper pattern for SEW PUZZLED.

PHOTO: JIM ALEXANDER NEWBERRY

Preparation

■ Finding Ideas

■ Developing Ideas

■ Supplies

■ Equipment

17

PREPARATION

Each time I lecture or teach a class, inevitably one of the first questions I'm asked is where I get my ideas. A better question might be, how I get my ideas. You won't like the answer though…anywhere and everywhere. I wish there was a formula I could pass on, and use myself when I'm stuck!!

The reality is that, as with any of our other talents, we need practice to sharpen our skills. According to the dictionary, one definition of the word "idea" is "thought." Thought is required to conceive ideas. Let's examine ways of finding and developing ideas.

■ Finding Ideas ■

Over and over, I hear students moan…but I don't have any good ideas! Of course you do; you just don't know it. Consider this…it's nearly supper time and you have no idea what to make. What do you do! You go to the cupboard or refrigerator, look at your options, and decide. Approaching fiber arts is really no different. The options may not be lying exposed on a shelf, but finding them isn't a mystery if you learn how, I encourage you to keep an open mind, and learn to recognize an idea and take control of it.

THEME OR SUBJECT

Reflecting on the body of work I've accumulated, it's evident I use themes as a starting point for my ideas. First let me say, my projects include no political statements and have no social significance, and I didn't dream them! Humorous and whimsical are descriptions often attributed to my pieces. Naturally, many issues in this world are of great concern to me; I just don't tend to deal with them through my sewing endeavors. Seeing the comical side of topics is the way my mind works. Usually, my pieces are a result of brainstorming a subject to death. My approach is a reflection of my interests and experiences, which has evolved into a personal style. Your own background will influence your choices. Allow yourself the time and freedom to find your own path!

Here are some theme ideas for you to consider featuring in an upcoming project.

- Holidays – provide an instant subject that helps narrow fabric choices: red & green for Christmas, orange & black for Halloween.
- Occasions or celebrations – birthdays, anniversaries, graduations, promotions, weddings, baby showers.
- Memory – in memory of a loved one, to remember something special like a trip or an outing, to mark a period of time like childhood, or college.
- Personalize – tell the world something about yourself: your family, your pets, a collection, or a hobby…if you have any other than sewing!
- Special crusades – save the whales, political, or social views.
- Gifts – thank you, welcome home, or farewell.
- Pictures or paintings.
- Favorite quilt patterns.
- Specific color or color combinations.
- Gardening or nature.
- Music.
- Sports.
- Animals.

Now let's look at some examples of how these ordinary themes or subjects found their way into my work.

OCCASION

I was asked to make a quilt to mark the occasion of a combination birthday and wedding anniversary party honoring my husband's parents. My idea to use our immediate family members as the theme seemed appropriate. Since I hadn't been quilting very long, my limited skills defined the direction of the piece. Lacking the talent to draw an original design and the experience to adequately appliqué, I decided to purchase a commercial pattern featuring pieced blocks. With one exception, I pieced the "figure blocks" as directed, depicting the personality of each through the clothing style and fabric choices. The ideas for the various embellishments came about through my analyzing each individual's lifestyle. This proved to be great fun and was a wonderful learning experience.

RIGHT: **FAMILY ALBUM QUILT, 32" x 39", 1988.**
Collection of Dr. & Mrs. William J. Micheels.
PHOTO: CHARLEY LYNCH

CHALLENGE

The "Go Fly a Kite" Challenge held during the 1989 American Quilter's Society Show led to another idea. Quiltmakers were challenged to create kites (they didn't actually have to fly), which would be suspended from the entryway ceiling at the show. Even though I'd never entered a contest before, the challenge was so intriguing I decided to try. Kites, kites, what would make an interesting kite! Have you ever heard the phrase, "If pigs could fly?" I'd run across this term and it kept running through my mind. I'm partial to cows, so what if the kite was made to resemble a cow instead of a pig! Finally I'd found an idea! The theme of the challenge was kites, but my subject was a Holstein cow. Okay, the first decision was made. Ideas can be thought of as decisions. If the kite was a cow, shouldn't it be able to fly! Having wings would help. …Oh, what a good decision! It might be sunny…better equip it with sunglasses…super idea! For a bit of humor I'd add pearls and sneakers to complete the attire. One of the challenge rules helped generate the idea of quilting the wings with metallic thread – the kite was required to have three layers and be quilted. A challenge can often present you with a theme while the rules may provide additional ideas.

CARTOON, DRAWING OR ARTWORK

A friend sent me a drawing of a cow lying on a psychiatrist's couch. The caption below said, "Maybe it's not me, y'know! Maybe it's the rest of the herd that's gone insane." In an instant I found an idea – I'd use a similar setting in a quilt. Given my fondness for bovines the idea of spotlighting a cow was appealing, but the plump female doctor in the cartoon kept grabbing my attention. I could easily picture her as a quilter, lying in a prone position, seeking help. Since we all know quilters are considered a tad compulsive, my next decision was to feature the neurosis being treated. I had no trouble relating! The border treatment required considerable thought, but when the idea to use crazy patch dawned, I couldn't believe it had taken me so long to think of it!

You don't have to wait for someone to send you a drawing in order to be motivated. Look around; you're surrounded by artwork; don't let it go unnoticed. I urge you to take time to discover the resources available in your area. Libraries, museums, art galleries, books, magazines, and newspapers are all wonderful depositories of potential ideas.

BELOW: **BUT, DOCTOR!**, 24" x 24", 1993. Collection of Ginger Createau. (Detail, page 91, top.)
PHOTO: RICHARD WALKER

JOURNAL

With all these ideas you'll need a way to keep track of your thoughts. A notebook, folder, or journal is a big help. I used to think I'd remember a good idea; now I know that's unlikely unless it's written down. Actually I have two journals. A small one is kept in my purse specifically for the purpose of jotting down ideas as they come. The other is a series of folders used to store visual aids (pic-tures, drawings, ads, etc.) that have been clipped for future reference. I know this smacks of being organized. I'm not a fanatic, but every once in a while the piles that have been deposited on every surface in my sewing room are scooped up and filed away in an attempt to make some kind of order. This has become a valuable habit that helps keep my scattered thoughts organized. I strongly recommend beginning a journal!

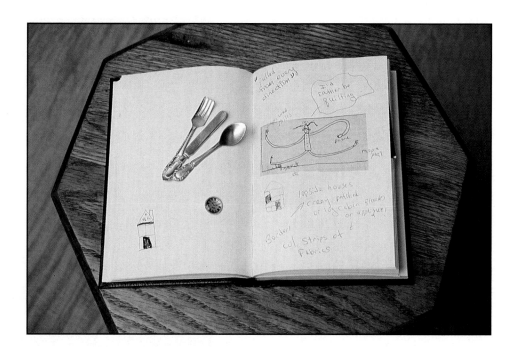

LEFT: The journal entry that was the inspiration for my wall quilt PULLED FROM EVERY DIRECTION.   PHOTO: JIM ALEXANDER NEWBERRY

BELOW: **PULLED FROM EVERY DIRECTION,** 38" x 38", 1994. (Full view, page 39; detail, page 91, bottom.)   PHOTO: RICHARD WALKER

■ Developing Ideas ■

You've just been versed in the mixture of ways I find ideas. The next step is to commit to the general idea and begin to develop it. Again this sounds far more complicated than the reality of the process. If I've said it once, I've repeated it a thousand times to my students, "Take one step at a time!"

TAKE ONE STEP AT A TIME

By reviewing the development of one of my favorite themes, you'll better understand how ideas flourish. My husband has collected cow creamers for years, accumulating about 130. You know the kind – a ceramic cow dispenses cream from its mouth, and we all know that's not what mother nature intended! Perhaps I was susceptible to all that bovine influence, because like my husband, I grew up in Wisconsin.

My own interest in the subject of cows began innocently enough when I purchased three ceramic cow buttons, for what I consid-

ered a rather hefty price of $12. I can't imagine what I was thinking since I didn't have a clue how to even make a buttonhole! My fear of learning was greater than my need to use them as originally intended, so I tried to think of another way of incorporating them. I remembered being amused by a quilt at a slide lecture which had cows floating in the clouds above the pasture. My decision to attach wings to the buttons, making a "cow heaven" avoided buttonholes altogether. A jacket featuring cow puns wasn't my original intent. That concept grew from the notion of featuring the buttons as "cow heaven," not as closures. So what else could I do – perhaps a purple cow…then a holy cow with a rhinestone halo…how about the cow that jumped over the moon! I think you follow the transition that took place. All ideas may not come at once – that's okay; just take one idea at a time!

However, the opposite may happen. You may have too many ideas! Often when I'm teaching, I see students try to put every idea they ever had into one project. The desire to use grandmother's lace as a theme is super, but it would be a shame to diminish the impact by adding that treasured collection of pastel Southwestern fabric. Staying in focus is easier when you realize this isn't the last project you'll ever make!

BE PATIENT

One factor I've noticed we all have to deal with is our impatience. None of us have nearly enough time to complete all the projects we'd like. So unfortunately, we often don't allow enough time for the thought process, which is especially necessary when creating original work. It's absolutely essential to remember that it takes time to design your own projects! Of course, at first you may be enthusiastic about the process, but as time passes the procedure may drag, and you'll need to remind yourself not to get anxious. Then comes the execution. Your plan may not conform to familiar sewing methods. Again, patience is required. More times than I care to recall, I've wasted three or four hours trying a new direction or technique that simply didn't work. Of course, time spent experimenting shouldn't be considered wasted. Yet we draw that conclusion because we usually don't have enough time to be

LEFT: **COW JACKET, 1988.**

PHOTO: RICHARD WALKER

27

generous with it! Don't let it get you down. Your next one-of-a-kind project will be your reward! If an unrealistic timetable is established, chances are you'll be in for a frustrating time. This is supposed to be fun! Take your time, let your work develop, and enjoy the process so you can enjoy the results.

PRACTICE

When I began quiltmaking, I made traditional patterns. The truth is, I not only couldn't imagine making "art quilts," I couldn't figure out why anybody would want to. My growing interest in wearables was the driving force behind my desire to create original work. It wasn't long before my quilts, too, showed the influence of an open mind. Of course, I wouldn't presume to tell you this doesn't require practice. Many quiltmakers, professional and hobbyist alike, have worked in a series. I used to roll my eyes upon hearing a remark in reference to "the fifth in a series." What's that all about! The answer is practice. Working within a somewhat con-

fined game plan makes you become more familiar and less timid with the procedures. You may be surprised to find you've stopped concentrating and fretting over some of the aspects that previously held your undivided attention. I know this sounds quite analytical, but experience has me convinced that practice strengthens skills and "frees your brain" to develop new ideas.

SOLICIT HELP

No one said you have to do this all by yourself. I thank my lucky stars that I have a super group of sewing pals! When mentally tapped out on a project, and whimpering like a baby, one of my talented friends is sure to offer another direction that may provide my solution. Guilds, quilt shops, and sewing centers provide other avenues. Sometimes I press my family members for opinions: "Do you like this, or is this one better?" They are brutally honest, so I'm always prepared in case the answer is a disappointing "neither." Don't be afraid to seek help!

RIGHT: **YARD ART MEMORIAL PARK, detail.** **The water in the bird bath was created by using blue sequin fabric. (Full view, page 73; detail, page 74.)**

PHOTO: RICHARD WALKER

■ Supplies ■

Interest in the subject of embellishments usually comes from those who have had experience sewing either quilts or garments. Therefore, I'm assuming the reader already has basic sewing supplies on hand. I will be introducing you to some of the tools and products that I have found useful which you may not have in your sewing room. The right tools not only speed up your work and improve your accuracy, but also make your task easier.

Some products are mentioned by generic terms, such as freezer paper; others are noted by the manufacturer's trade name. I've had success with these specific articles and feel comfortable recommending them. There may be alternatives to the products specifically identified; feel free to substitute. For your convenience, a list of mail order sources is included on page 30.

•Fabrics that are readily available are a huge advantage. Most of us have a stash on which we can rely, so I hardly need to mention this mandatory ingredient. The merits of having an assortment on hand will be evident the first time you have to stop what you're doing to run out and search for the perfect "snow" fabric. My collection was quite meager at first, not only in size but also in variety. Thanks to a friend who rescued several large boxes of samples from a bankrupt dressmaker's dumpster, my collection has now expanded to include a little of everything from wool

SUPPLIERS

SECOND STORI
6 Coldren Dr.
Prospect Heights, IL 60070
(708) 870-1734
The Portable Freestanding Flannel Wall Kit® & Bow Whip Tools®

WEB OF THREAD
3240 Lone Oak Rd.
Paducah, KY 42003
1-800-955-8185
Specialty threads, yarn, ribbon, cords, and machine needles

NANCY'S NOTIONS
333 Beichl Ave.
P.O. Box 683
Beaver Dam, WI 53916-0683
1-800-833-0690
June Tailor products, general sewing supplies

PELLE'S SEE-THRU STAMPS
P.O. Box 242
Davenport, CA 95017
Phone/Fax: (408) 425-4743
Stamps, stamp pads, and ink

CLOTILDE
1909 S.W. First Ave.
Fort Lauderdale, FL 33315-2100
1-800-772-2891
Beacon® glue products

CREATIVE BEGINNINGS
475 Morro Bay Blvd.
Morro Bay, CA 93442
1-800-992-0276
Charms, trinkets

to silk. Another pal saves me samples from a decorating firm. The majority of the material I use is still 100% cotton, including unbleached muslin for foundations. Experiment to find a brand of muslin that doesn't turn into a mass of permanent wrinkles that can't be removed, even by a steamroller.

•Newsprint can be purchased very inexpensively from many newspaper printers. I can purchase an end roll that lasts me about six months for a few dollars. The size and cost of the paper make it a practical choice for drawing designs.

•Freezer paper has become indispensible to quilters. We are finding more and more uses for this product. Purchase it in your supermarket or try restaurant supply stores that carry larger and wider rolls. Polycoated paper placed shiny side down on fabric will adhere when pressed with a warm iron. Freezer paper can act as a stabilizer, template, or sewing guide.

•Marking pencils and pens need to be tested for ease of removability. The type of embellishing explored in this book generally does not permit the laundering methods we are accustomed to. In areas where markings may be visible, use a product such as chalk, one that brushes away easily.

•Embroidery scissors are necessary to trim excess fabric from sewn seams. I use the small pointed type most often to trim appliqué edges, and to clip corners and curves.

•Turning tools help you turn sewn faced shapes to the right side, and assist when stuffing them. The brand I like to use for my 3-D appliqué embellishment projects is the Bow Whip®.

•Flex-a-Curve® bends to a desired shape and holds its shape until you change it to another design. It's useful for drawing freeform curves that need to be repeated.

•Fabric value filter enables you to determine the difference in value (lightness or darkness) of fabric, without confusing your eye with the color. I use this inexpensive hand-held, see-through plastic paddle regularly.

•Pattern weights hold patterns of all types to fabric, saving the time and trouble of pinning. I like the versatility of the Quilting-Wate® set by June Tailor because each weight is a different shape. The narrow one, for instance, fits nicely on smaller pattern pieces like a collar.

•Cut 'n Press® by June Tailor has become a real favorite with me. I use it as a lap board to support my appliqué projects. The cushioned side (pressing side) rests on my lap, while the hard (cutting surface) is on top. I'm getting better results using this rather unconventional method of appliqué because it gives me a place to rest my hand while I sew, and provides a surface on which to smooth out my work from time to time. Of course, you could always use it as a portable cutting and pressing surface, as originally intended!

•Press mitt is my solution to the often challenging task of pressing completed 3-D garments. With it, my hand becomes the ironing surface, making smaller areas accessible to the iron. This is another product from June Tailor, who has definitely made my life easier.

•Fabric glues are an option when sewing an embellishment is impractical or impossible. FABRI TAC®, GEM TAC®, and LIQUI FUSE®, all by Beacon, can be purchased in most full service fabric or craft stores. Always read the label and experiment with the glue on identical or nearly identical surfaces, before attempting to use it on a project.

■ Equipment ■

•Good lighting is a must! In addition to the obvious danger of using a rotary cutter when you can't see where you're cutting, straining to see causes fatigue. This item is listed first to emphasize how critical I view decent lighting to be.

•Sewing machine in good working order. It isn't necessary to possess the top of the line machine, but it is mandatory to have one that performs properly. Owning a machine which has as many features as your budget allows, plus keeping it in good working order, will be one of the wisest investments you can make. Some of the features I have found to be particularly useful for my projects are a built in walking foot, a "needle down" button, programmed embroidery stitches, and a variety of alphabet styles for lettering.

•Light box to aid when tracing designs. Until recently, I taped designs to my patio window to trace. A light box is so much more convenient and accurate. And you don't have to wait for the daylight! Light boxes can be purchased in some quilt and fabric shops, in most craft, drafting, or art supply stores, and through many mail order firms. A friend's large glass dining table became a substitute light box for me while I was marking a large whole cloth quilt. By taping the purchased pattern to the table and positioning the quilt top to cover the design, the light of a lamp (minus its shade) placed on the floor under the table made the lines clearly visible to trace. Another alternative is to rig your own light box. Place any light source in a box (even cardboard will do), and cover with a piece of clear plexiglass which can be purchased in most hardware stores.

•Dress form in your size is helpful. One of the factors to be considered when adding embellishments to garments is wearability. The placement of embellishments is important. You probably wouldn't, for example, want to dangle a trinket in the center of a breast. Fitting the garment on a dress form should help you avoid such dangers. (Your own body and a mirror would work too!)

•Design wall to help you plan your work, like the ones many professional quiltmakers use when creating quilts. Getting my work up off the living room floor has helped improve my designs by allowing me to get the proper perspective. Many of us don't have the luxury of a spare wall to use. The Portable Free-Standing Flannel Wall® kit allows you to build one to suit your space. I've found it immensely beneficial when designing my 3-D scenic quilts.

Chapter Three

ABOVE: BOO!, detail. (Front view, page 35; back view, page 70; details, page 70, 83.)

PHOTO: RICHARD WALKER

ABOVE: BOO!, front view, 1992. (Back view, page 70; details, page 34, 70, 83.)

Background Designs

- ■ General Construction Guidelines
- ■ Plain Background
- ■ Hand Appliquéd – Dual Background
- ■ Hand Appliquéd – Complete Background
- ■ Machine Appliquéd Background
- ■ Pieced Background
- ■ Background Pieced on a Foundation

BACKGROUND DESIGNS

By now I imagine your fingers are itching to grab a needle and start sewing. Good! Ah, but what are you going to embellish! Rather than sewing a garment or quilt and then trying to figure out how to embellish it, my approach is to design and construct a "background" geared to the type of embellishments I have in mind.

First I must judge the size, scale, color, and even the weight of the articles to be added in order to select a properly constructed background. What articles you might ask! Well remember, I've already established an idea or theme and am prepared to proceed. Even if I don't have every detail planned, I know the general direction.

Unfortunately, even though my sewing room is well equipped I can't call out an order for a prepared background and expect to pick it up in an hour. Translating ideas from the mind to fabric requires slightly more dedication.

Please don't start wringing your hands. If all you want to do for now is embellish a completed project, you can! This segment will guide you toward compatible choices of embellishments by familiarizing you with various types of construction. Furthermore, if in the future you decide to design a background for a specific embellishment method, you will know how!

Keep in mind, if the embellishment is the star of the show, the background of your piece should be exactly that – a background. It should complement the overall plan, rather than being a source of distraction. Certainly, the time spent creating embellishments will be squandered if the background overwhelms your hard work.

LEFT: **AND SO THEY WERE MOORRIED,** detail.
(Front and back view, page 5.)
PHOTO: JIM ALEXANDER NEWBERRY

■ General Construction Guidelines ■

Whether making a quilt or a garment, I generally make my background larger than the planned finished size. During the process of appliquéing, quilting, beading, and even embroidering, these background pieces can "shrink" considerably. I control the size of my backgrounds by completing as much embellishing as possible before the garment piece or quilt is cut to size. I'm careful to keep the design elements simple and expendable for at least an inch around the perimeter so no matter how much or how little cutting is done to achieve the proper size, I won't have to sacrifice any important details of my plan.

QUILTS: Unless a specific finished size is required, quilts tend to allow the maker some leeway in the size. Since my quilts do not involve the structured patchwork block normally associated with quiltmaking, they're relatively easy to plan. As long as the quilt is flat and square, I'm not usually concerned whether the piece ends up 49 inches square, or the planned 50 inches. I do,

though, take some precautions which help me get as close as possible to the desired finished size. If I want a finished 50 inch square quilt, all my cutting and sewing dimensions will be geared to make it a 51 inch top. This figure can be adjusted according to the amount of appliqué, quilting, and embellishing planned. My working figures for a quilt that will only have a meager amount of quilting and embellishing, might be 50½ inches instead. If pieced borders are planned, I try to select a pattern that can be trimmed without altering the design or quality of workmanship. Chopping off an unwanted ½ inch of a crazy patch border is possible, but eliminating the points that make up a saw-tooth border would be terrible. Here's another approach I use when making my scenic 3-D quilts with pieced borders: I add the extra ½ inch – 1 inch total – to the outer edges of the scenic design, basically treating that area as though it were a separate quilt. I complete as much of the work as possible, square it to size, and then add the borders.

GARMENTS: I do every bit of quilting and embellishing possible before the pieces are sewn together. My preferred method is to mark each major pattern piece on a rectangular piece of fabric, large enough to allow a margin of several inches around all areas of the pattern. Here are the advantages: 1) The pattern piece is cut out after all necessary handling, helping you avoid the possibility of stretching and distorting the bias edges in areas such as the neck. 2) The boundaries of the area to be embellished are apparent without your having to deal with cut edges that could unravel or fray. 3) Flat rectangles of fabric are easier to handle. 4) The excess fabric is helpful when you are securing the work in quilting or embroidery hoops. 5) Most importantly, when you finally cut a pattern piece to the correct size, you don't have to worry about how much the piece has shrunk during embellishing. You know you'll have an adequate amount.

■ Plain Backgrounds ■

My definition of a plain background is a simple unadorned base with which to begin. One of the advantages I like best about this type of background is that there is little or no piecing preparation. You are free to begin embellishing almost immediately. Generally, by "plain" I'm referring to fashion fabric, not muslin. However, using muslin as a background to showcase a collection of beautiful vintage lace would guarantee success. Plain doesn't necessarily mean a solid fabric, although, if a print is used, it should "read" solid, since the purpose of a plain background is to allow attention to be focused on the embellishments.

The type of embellishments planned will have a major impact on the construction procedure used. Typically, it's necessary to use a foundation such as muslin, batting, or fusible interfacing to add support to the background if the fabric is a light or medium weight cotton. The weight of the embellishments you are adding will affect how the garment or quilt hangs. Fabrics such as heavier weights of corduroy, denim, or cotton sheeting may be suitable for some applications without the necessity of a foundation. Let's examine two projects with plain backgrounds that utilize different construction methods in order to accommodate the selected embellishments.

EXAMPLES

RIGHT, TOP: **MARY, MARY, HOW DOES YOUR GARDEN GROW? WHY WITH FABRIC, OF COURSE! #1**, back view, 1991. (Detail, page 77.)
PHOTO: RICHARD WALKER

I lightly marked my bodice pattern piece, in my correct size, on a rectangle of gold 100% cotton fabric and thread basted a rectangle of muslin to the wrong side. The design elements were hand appliquéd in place through both layers, allowing the muslin to help stabilize the work. I retraced my pattern piece, cut it out, and sewed the jumper.

RIGHT, BOTTOM: **PULLED FROM EVERY DIRECTION**, full view. (Full view, page 25; detail, page 91.)
PHOTO: RICHARD WALKER

From the conception of this project I knew my focal point, the stuffed figure, would be bulky and heavy – and require stabilizing. Many of the miniatures I had would also need a solid foundation, yet the homespun fabric I selected wasn't suitable to be used by itself. I devised a plan! The quilt top was stitched and basted together with Fairfield's Cotton Classic® batting, which stabilized it for the appliqué and embellishing process. Some embellishments such as the iron, book, and mouse trap were glued to the quilt after it was quilted, squared, and bound.

■ Hand Appliqué – Dual Background ■

This method is the one I use most often to create a scene or a setting for my 3-D garments. Selected fabrics which depict the scene are hand appliquéd to a portion of fashion fabric. This presents a dual background, part appliqué and part plain. The fashion fabric could also be considered a foundation in this case. Since I generally don't cut away the fashion fabric from behind the appliqué, I watch for any shadowing that may occur, before it becomes a problem. Shadowing occurs when the presence of fabric (usually a darker color behind a lighter one) can be seen or detected. Trimming the offending fabric's seam allowance shorter than the other can solve that distracting and unattractive problem. By leaving the foundation (fashion fabric) in place, I retain the weight necessary to support my 3-D shapes. These tips will assist you in creating a garment with a hand appliquéd – dual background.

•Transfer the garment pattern, one size larger than you normally wear, to a large sheet of paper (blank newsprint is perfect). Sketch the scene. Note: If the design is very simple and only a few 3-D elements are planned, you can work in your correct size.

• Mark the garment pattern, one size larger than you normally wear, on a rectangle fashion fabric. Don't cut at this time.

• Cut the scenic shapes from the paper pattern. Use them as templates to mark and cut your selected fabrics. Adding a generous seam allowance of ¼" will give you a margin of error. Excess fabric can always be trimmed; it can't be added!

• Baste in position on the fashion fabric. Following the steps below will allow the seam allowances to be trimmed as you work:

1. Lay out the marked rectangle of the fashion fabric with right side facing you.

2. Working from the bottom up, lay the **second** strip of the scene in position. Always add the strips with right sides facing you.

3. Place bottom of the scene – the **first** strip – in place.

4. Baste **top** edge of the first strip (the edge you will be appliquéing). Fold the strip up and trim excess seam allowance underneath. Reposition this bottom piece and baste bottom and side edges to the foundation fashion fabric. The basting will secure this strip, so it won't get in the way while you are completing the design.

5. Now take the **third** from the bottom piece and baste the **bottom** edge (the edge you will be appliquéing). Fold down, trim seam allowance if necessary, and reposition piece.

6. Take the **fourth** piece and repeat process as completed for third strip.

7. Repeat until design is completed.

8. Appliqué, using thread to match each fabric.

When all the designing and embellishing is completed, re-mark the pattern pieces, using your correct size, and cut out. (Because of the appliqué and the embellishing process, the original larger size markings may be just about one size smaller at this time.) I generally don't quilt these garments, but if you wish to quilt yours, baste batting in place, quilt, and then cut to size.

■ Hand Appliqué – Complete Background ■

This procedure works equally well for garments and quilts. Fabrics are appliquéd onto a muslin foundation, creating a background to embellish. Drawing a full size design is helpful, but not always necessary. If the desired background is to be scenic, consisting of appliquéd foreground details, it is helpful to sketch the design. This sketch will direct the size and scale of the rest of the components. The drawing can be utilized as a pattern and traced onto the muslin to guide in fabric placement, or it can be cut apart and used as templates.

Sometimes all you wish to achieve is a neutral background, not a scene. You can cut random pieces of similar fabrics and treat them like a puzzle. This method provides a quick background that requires no templates, since you have the option of cutting away the muslin and trimming the seam allowances.

When making quilts, I pin the traced muslin foundation or the paper pattern to my Portable Free-Standing Flannel Wall® and audition fabrics. I drape fabric possibilities on my dress form for garment designs. Viewing these fabrics through a value filter helps me determine which combinations will work together. Sometimes it takes me almost as long to prepare the design, select the fabrics, and cut them for appliquéing as it does for the actual sewing of the entire background. Over-analyzing a project doesn't necessarily result in a better scheme. Try to follow your instincts. I'm always preaching to my students: "Take one step at a time." All this preparation is necessary, so enjoy the process!"

EXAMPLE
BELOW: **BACON AND EGGS, 57" x 53", 1993. Example – hand appliqué, complete background.**
PHOTO: JIM ALEXANDER NEWBERRY

This quilt-in-progress was made using paper templates and has been hand appliquéd to a muslin foundation. The edges will be trimmed after all the surface designing is complete and the quilting finished.

Once an appliqué background is completed, I cut the muslin backing away with sharp embroidery scissors, trimming seam allowances if necessary. Next the piece is embellished as fully as possible. For quilt-making, thread basting the top together with batting and backing and hand quilting the layers provides the necessary long-term stability for the embellishments.

Garments are treated in a similar manner, except I eliminate adding a backing fabric. The garment's lining will cover and protect the batting after it's quilted.

EXAMPLE

BELOW: **ARE THE STREETS IN HEAVEN REALLY PAVED WITH FABRIC?**, front view, 1991. (Back view, page 61; details, page 61, 71, 78.)
PHOTO: courtesy of QUILTER'S NEWSLETTER MAGAZINE

The blue background was created by randomly hand appliquéing the fabric to marked muslin rectangles. After the muslin was cut away and seam allowances trimmed, lighter weight embellishments, other appliqué designs, and embroidery details were added. Next, batting was basted to the wrong side and hand quilted. The remaining embellishments were added and the pattern pieces were re-marked and cut out. Finally, the jacket was sewn together and the lining added.

■ Machine Appliquéd Background ■

Machine appliqué is a technique I use sparingly for my projects because I prefer the look of hand appliqué. But there have been times when I've decided to add some details to a prepared background using this method. Utilizing the sewing machine to appliqué a design onto a heavy denim background certainly has advantages. Some sewers love machine appliqué because they feel it's quicker than the hand work required to achieve the same results. I've seen exquisite examples of machine work that anyone would be proud to claim. Your comfort level executing this process should be your guide. As always, I encourage you to experiment. Though this isn't my path, it may be yours!

I recommend using fusible webbing to bond the shapes to the background fabric, before machine appliquéing. This prevents movement of the design, resulting in pucker-free appliqué. Recently, lighter weight webbing products have become available which help to reduce the stiffness of appliqué designs, one of the objections I had to this method.

EXAMPLE

BELOW: **PEAKY AND SPIKE – DOWN ON THE FARM.** Front view, 1990. (Details, page 58, 71.)
PHOTO: MARY STORI

The garment was made using the dual appliqué background construction process. Even though the fashion fabric was only a medium weight chambray, the scenic fabrics, many of them fused and machine appliquéd, were enough to stabilize the shirt for the 3-D embellishing.

■ Pieced Background ■

Have you ever sewn a quilt block! If the answer is yes, you already possess the skills you need to prepare a pieced background. Don't despair if you answered in the negative; there's nothing to it. The idea is to create your own "yardage" by sewing smaller pieces of fabric together in a planned or random fashion. I prefer machine piecing, which not only delivers faster results, but also offers greater durability.

You may already have pieced yardage somewhere in your stack of unfinished projects. What about that quilt top (or partial top) that for whatever reason never made it beyond that stage! Consider cutting garment pattern pieces from this ready-made yardage.

A real luxury would be having ample yardage to allow the garment pieces to be arranged on the quilt top so you could take advantage of the pieced pattern.

Perhaps your top quilt top includes sashing strips between the blocks. Explore the design possibilities these present. Try laying a sleeve pattern on the quilt top so that it incorporates a sashing band at the wrist, or down the length of the sleeve. Do you have blocks left over from a completed quilt! Dig in your stash for complementary fabric and piece some yardage. Where are the patches you've squirreled away from that project you abandoned two years ago! Recycle them!

EXAMPLE

LEFT: **TIC-TAC COLOR BLOCK, front view, 1991.**
Pieced background. (Detail, page 87.)

PHOTO: RICHARD WALKER

A purchased fabric package was the inspiration for this quickly pieced garment. I loved the way these 100% solid cotton fabrics complemented each other. I added some solid black fabric to the group and assigned a different color to each section of the jacket. This was so straight forward that it wasn't even necessary to draw a diagram. By referring to my jacket pattern, I was able to roughly measure the size of each of the color block sections I'd envisioned. The appropriate fabric color was cut into large rectangles or squares and stitched together. Exact measurements of each color block section weren't critical since my pattern featured dolman sleeves (sleeves cut-in-one with the jacket). My aim was to sew one large pieced square for the back, and two pieced rectangles for the front. Next, I traced the pattern pieces on my prepared fabric, marked quilting lines, thread basted batting to each piece, and quilted it.

My planned background was the pieced color-blocked fashion fabric. The hand quilting was a supplementary planned design. Even though I'd used black thread for the quilting, the impact was rather blah, certainly less than desired! Remember what I said? I know the general direction in which I want a garment to develop, but not every detail can be planned. The addition of black trim and beads saved this piece, and fortunately the batting that was already in place provided adequate support for the beadwork! Finally, satisfied with my background and the unexpected embellishments, I re-marked the pieced rectangles with the garment pattern pieces, cut them out, and finished constructing the garment. Because I worked on a rectangle (or square), ample fabric was available to accommodate the "shrinkage" of both the quilting and the unplanned beading. Remember, you are the designer. Don't be afraid to proceed in a manner that makes sense for the undertaking at hand!

■ Background Pieced on a Foundation ■

The only difference between this method and the pieced background already described is that with this method the pieced fabric is pieced onto a foundation. This construction method is the one used quite often for crazy patch piecing. Single pieces of fabric or individual blocks can be sewn in random or orderly fashion to a foundation of muslin. This type of background is useful when you need to add strength or sturdiness to the fashion fabric. It's a good alternative to batting because it isn't as heavy or bulky and quilting isn't necessary. Sew using a ¼ inch seam allowance and whenever possible, press seams open to reduce bulk.

EXAMPLE

RIGHT: **THREE EWES AND A MOO**, front view, **1991. Background pieced on a foundation.**
PHOTO: RICHARD WALKER

The front and back bodice pattern pieces were traced onto sheets of blank newsprint. Each was divided into various size sections. A rectangular piece of muslin was placed over each paper pattern and all the lines were traced. Using what I call the "paint by number" system, I designed, cut, and sewed one section at a time, laying each in its proper position on the paper pattern. This process served two purposes: 1) I was able to evaluate the background's design as it developed. 2) It allowed me to confirm the sizes of the "blocks" were correct. When I was satisfied with all elements, I sewed the sections to the marked muslin and added the stuffed 3-D pieces.

■ A Final Word ■

Now that you are more familiar with the variety of backgrounds I've found useful for my projects, you are ready to begin your own experimenting. Remember, I've presented guidelines, not rules. As you have learned, each project takes on its own personality and its own problems. By regarding them as challenges rather than obstacles, I learn something new every time – you will too!

Chapter Four

ABOVE: MARY, MARY, HOW DOES YOUR GARDEN GROW? WHY WITH FABRIC, OF COURSE! #2, detail front view, 1992. Narrow fabric tubes are gathered over thin cotton cording (ruched) and hand stitched to the jumper bodice to divide the sections of this "flower garden." (Details, pages 15, 52, 59.)

PHOTO: RICHARD WALKER

Embellishing Methods

- ■ Stuffed 3-D Appliqué
- ■ Traditional Hand Appliqué
- ■ Fabric Manipulation
- ■ Hand Quilting
- ■ Hand Embroidery
- ■ Lettering
- ■ Specialty Threads & Materials
- ■ Ribbon, Trim, Cording, & Piping
- ■ Lace
- ■ Specialty Fabric
- ■ Paints
- ■ Patches
- ■ Beads
- ■ Buttons, Charms, Trinkets, Pins & Costume Jewelry
- ■ Miniatures
- ■ Oddities

EMBELLISHING METHODS

Planning, analyzing, and problem solving are all integral parts of creating embellished artwork. I've stressed the importance of compatibility between the surface designs and the background. For each of the embellishing methods covered in this chapter, you'll find recommendations to assist you in making appropriate background construction choices.

Some of the techniques are unorthodox; others are common. You'll discover many surface design methods are easier to add before the construction process is complete; others work well as afterthoughts. I strive to create well designed pieces, using a variety of methods that are pleasing from a distance, yet invite the viewer for a closer inspection. If you develop a particular fondness for any one type of design, be assured you'll have no trouble locating books pertaining to specific subjects, such as beading or embroidery, which can help you widen your knowledge. Experiment with these methods. Enjoy yourself and have fun creating your own one-of-a-kind embellished artwork!

CLASSIFICATION OF BACKGROUND CONSTRUCTION MATERIALS

•**lightweight** – one layer of woven fashion fabric such as: 100% cotton (calicoes, large prints, homespun, and solids), Chambray, Madras, and most of the plaid, check, and stripe collections found in quilt shops under well known names such as Marcus Brothers, Red Wagon, Roberta Horton, Fons-Porter Heritage Collection, Mission Valley Folk Art Plaids. "Lightweight" does not refer to polyester/cotton blends intended for dressmaking, polyester silkies, rayon, silk, satin, metallics, lamés, or sheer fabrics.

•**medium weight** – one layer of firmly woven or sturdy fashion fabric such as 100% cotton sheeting, poplin, denim, wool, and corduroy.

•**stabilized** – one layer lightweight or medium weight fashion fabric which is stabilized with a foundation such as another layer of fashion fabric, muslin, iron-on interfacing, or batting (I prefer Fairfield's Cotton Classic® or Hobbs Bonded Fibers Thermore®).

Note: These are guidelines! The biggest factor to consider when matching embellishments to background is the weight of the surface design. Here's an example – you've decided to add some beads to an isolated area of a garment. Choosing a lightweight background might seem fine, and probably would be if you were using seed beads. But if the beads are large, heavy, and closely concentrated, a better choice would a medium or stabilized fabric which would help offset the uneven weight in the surrounding areas.

■ Stuffed 3-D Appliqué ■

Background requirement – medium weight or stabilized.

My work often utilizes a method I've developed and dubbed "stuffed 3-D appliqué." It's my way to creatively avoid dealing with raw edges on small appliqué pieces. Browsing through this book, you'll find an assortment of shapes, sizes, and subjects that have been made as 3-D designs. Don't expect to achieve sharp points or the precision of hand appliqué with this technique. Luckily, it works perfectly for my whimsical folk art style. Follow the steps below to make your own stuffed 3-D shapes.

1. Draw or draft a shape on paper (graph, typing, freezer), or template plastic.

2. Place two pieces of fabric, right sides together, and trace the design on the wrong side of the top piece. The fabric must always be at least an inch larger than the design in every direction. This provides a small area of fabric you can use to guide the piece while sewing and prevents the fabric from getting caught in the throat plate of your machine while you're sewing.

3. Sew directly on the marked line using a very small stitch (I use 1.0). Thread should match the fabric. Stitch completely around the shape, stopping about ⅛" beyond the starting point. TIPS: Cut freezer paper into the desired shape, press to the wrong side of fabric (shiny side toward fabric), sew just outside the paper's edge. An open or no-bridge embroidery foot allows a better view of the design line.

4. Cut out the sewn shape, using a ⅛" seam allowance. Clip any inside points or curves.

LEFT: **NOT QUITE SNOWBOUND**, detail of front. The snowmen, reindeer, dog, and some of the trees (2"-3" tall) are typical examples of stuffed 3-D appliqué. Notice some of the trees and the wagon have not been stuffed, though they are faced shapes. I think it is a little more interesting to vary the designs. (Full view, page 40; back view, page 55.)

PHOTO: RICHARD WALKER

BELOW: **NOT QUITE SNOWBOUND**, back view, 1990. The Christmas tree is a larger example of stuffed 3-D appliqué. Rather than being stuffing with polyester fill, the branches contain a thin layer of batting.

PHOTO: RICHARD WALKER

5. Using small, sharp embroidery scissors, cut a slash in the top layer, the side facing you as you've sewn. When turned you'll have a duplicate of your template. To reverse the shape – cut a slash in the bottom (back) layer.

6. With the aid of a turning tool, turn the shape inside out.

7. Stuff lightly with poly-stuffing and hand stitch the opening closed.

Look for theme fabrics to speed up the process. You'll find fabric printed with everything from hot dogs with mustard to bulldogs with sunglasses. The size of the subject matter will determine whether the fabric is potential 3-D material. Some shapes may be too intricate or too small to turn; others may be too big to use. Prepare these ready-made shapes as instructed above.

■ Traditional Hand Appliqué ■

Background requirement – lightweight, medium weight, or stabilized fabric. Appliqué shouldn't be heavier than the background.

Technically, traditional hand appliqué may not be considered surface design, but I'll take the liberty of including it. My approach is a little more relaxed than the standard methods since exact positioning isn't usually essential for my projects.

1. Draft or draw a shape on paper or template material and cut out.

2. Positioning it on the right side of fabric, trace a thin line around the shape. Cut out using a scant ¼" seam allowance.

3. Eyeball the correct position on the background and thread baste in place. I much prefer to take the time to thread baste rather than deal with pins sticking me while I work, especially if there's a lot of appliquéing to do!

4. Appliqué, needle turning the seam allowance at the marked line, using thread to match the fabric being appliquéd. Remove basting stitches.

TIP: For years I avoided appliqué because I was terrible at it! We all want to be immediate experts! Unfortunately appliqué takes practice. A trick that helped me improve my appliqué technique was to use a firm surface on my lap. I learned this quite by accident one day when I grabbed my June Tailor Quilter's Cut 'n Press Mat™ to help support a particularly heavy project I was working on. The board supported my hands and gave me a place to smooth out the work from time to time to confirm the fabric was even and flat. I haven't appliquéd without this board since!

RIGHT: **QUEEN OF HEARTS, back view, 1992. A 25-year-old, shi-sha mirrored Afghanistan embroidered panel was the inspiration for this long jacket. Traditional appliqué was used for most of the design components that create the playing card. The weight of this heavy garment was supported by my Cut 'n Press Mat™ as I stitched. (Front view, page 8; details, page 9, 69.)**

PHOTO: RICHARD WALKER

■ Fabric Manipulation ■

Background requirement – medium weight or stabilized fabric.

Dimension is easily achieved by folding, twisting, pleating, scrunching, or otherwise manipulating fabric. The possibilities this medium presents are stimulating, especially when you realize how little effort it takes! The examples below explain how to create a tree canopy and a caterpillar. By altering the fabric, size, and shape, the first technique will yield clouds, ponds, lakes, rivers, snow, mud, and bushes to name a few. Use the second to make flowers, leaves, insects, wings of birds, and whatever else your imagination suggests.

TREE CANOPY

1. Stitch a tree trunk to background fabric.
2. On paper, draw the shape of a mass of tree leaves in the finished size you need and cut out. Check the size and shape by placing the cutout on your project; redo if necessary. Lightly trace the outline of the final design in the desired position on the background.
3. Now pin the paper on the right side of a piece of green printed fabric. Using it as a guide, cut the fabric in approximately the same shape as the paper, but at least twice its size.
4. Position the fabric to fit inside the marked lines on the background. You'll need to scrunch and wrinkle up the fabric as you place it to make it fit. Don't worry about being too exact or tidy; nature isn't!
5. Hand appliqué to the background by turning the edges under about ⅛". The marked line on the background will be your shaping guide.
6. To secure the inside area of the tree canopy and maintain the wrinkled effect, take several stitches in place through all the layers in a number of places, until you achieve a pleasing effect.

TIP: The illusion of an apple tree can be made by sewing red wooden beads on the scrunched fabric. A multicolored print fabric featuring golds, reds, and browns would be a nice choice to depict a tree in the fall season.

CATERPILLAR

1. Cut one strip of print fabric ¾" wide x 6" long. If you want a fatter or longer caterpillar, adjust measurements.

2. With wrong side facing you, fold up the edges of the two short sides ¼" and press. Fold the two long edges together to meet and press.

3. Beginning at one short end, fold the strip accordion style, leaving the opposite end slightly longer to act as a head. Carefully (so you don't burn your fingers), steam press to help retain the shape. Pin or baste the caterpillar to the background, placing the seam toward the background fabric.

4. Hand appliqué, using matching thread. Embroider two French knots for eyes.

TIP: Even though it requires sewing through many fabric layers, it's easier to do the embroidery on pieces that are as small as the caterpillar after the pieces have been appliquéd in position.

■ Hand Quilting ■

Background requirement – stabilized fabric with batting.

Hand quilting enhances both garments and quilts with wonderful texture and design. I love to quilt; it's the part of a project I look forward to the most! It can be disconcerting to quilt around a lot of embellishments. After attempting to force pieces into a hoop without damaging the embellishments, I'm resigned to quilting them without the aid of a hoop or frame. Again, I recommend putting some type of lap board under your work to support the project so that from time to time you can spread it out to be sure the work is smooth and flat. When working on a large, heavy quilt, I sit on my couch with my legs resting on a big coffee table in front of me. By spreading the weight out to the front and on either side, I find the task easier to manage.

Quilting stitches can create the illusion of wind around a tornado, texture on a dirt road, and waves in the ocean. I use Sulky® variegated rayon thread (40 weight) to furnish the complex colors we see in nature, without the trouble of having to change threads. Many machine artists use this type of thread to add rich color and sheen to their work. While the effects of rayon thread aren't quite as dramatic when it is hand quilted, it still has the ability to reflect light and rewards the viewer with a little something extra! My students tend to

view rayon thread with trepidation because they have heard it isn't as strong and is difficult to handle. Not so! I've had wonderful success with Sulky® thread, as long as I refrain from cutting the piece longer than about 15 inches. If a thread starts to fray, I immediately tie it off and start a fresh one.

My first Fairfield Fashion Show garment, ARE THE STREETS IN HEAVEN REALLY PAVED WITH FABRIC?, was entirely quilted with a variegated Sulky® rayon thread, and after a year of frequent handling while it traveled with the show, my jacket came back in perfect condition!

Hand quilting can also be the design rather than a supporting element. A stipple quilted tuxedo ensemble with trapunto work became a three month labor of love! The quilting designs for each garment section were planned on paper patterns made one size larger than I normally wear and traced to rectangles of fashion fabric. Next batting and a muslin backing were basted to each marked piece. After the quilting and trapunto were completed, I retraced the garment pattern pieces using my correct size. When I discovered the "shrinkage" was greater than anticipated, I didn't have to hit the panic button since my method of working on a rectangle provided ample fabric!

Paper pattern and marked rectangle of fabric which has been basted in preparation for hand quilting.

PHOTO: MARY STORI

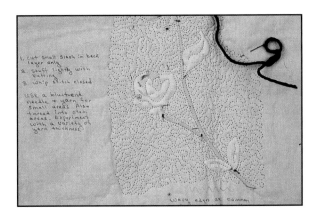

Wrong side of a fabric rectangle I use as a sample for my students. A portion of the stipple quilting and trapunto work has been completed.

PHOTO: MARY STORI

LEFT: **ONE O'CLOCK JUMP**, front & back view, 1990. This tuxedo ensemble is an example of the ultimate hand quilted whole cloth garment!

PHOTOS: BILL LEMPKE

Quilting detail.

PHOTO: BILL LEMPKE

■ Hand Embroidery ■

Background requirement – lightweight, medium weight, or stabilized fabric.

Embroidery stitches are an excellent way to create narrow details that are too small to piece or appliqué. Embroidery floss is available in every color imaginable. Try stitching with yarn, decorative serger threads, metallic threads, or ribbon floss to achieve interesting designs. This embellishment is extremely versatile; a French knot can represent an eye, several rows of outline stitches can suddenly become a spider web. The stem stitch is great for outlining and lettering. One strand of thread will create a delicate line; additional strands produce a more defined line. Always test the stitches on a scrap of fabric to check the density and color. Whenever possible, I secure the fabric in a hoop to maintain uniform tension.

You'll need practice to determine at what point to add embroidery. The overall design and composition of the piece will set the embellishing schedule for you – thinking through the order in which to proceed is a valuable habit to develop! Sometimes it's necessary to do the embroidery at the beginning of the project, as was the case when I made MR. McGREGOR'S FOLLY. Here's how I proceeded:

1. A dual-appliquéd background was prepared for the embroidery.

2. I assigned different vegetables to each area and drew thin chalk lines freehand, to represent vines, leaves, and roots.

3. Four strands of floss, each a different shade of the same color to mimic nature, were used, to provide greater definition to the various stitches, giving the appearance of plant material.

4. Once the plants were in place, the stuffed 3-D and embroidered vegetables were added.

RIGHT: MR. McGREGOR'S FOLLY, full front & detail, 1989. The brown vines of the potatoes and string bean plants were created using the stem stitch. This stitch was also used for the sun's rays, the tomato plant, and the stems of the flowers on the sleeve.

PHOTOS: RICHARD WALKER

64

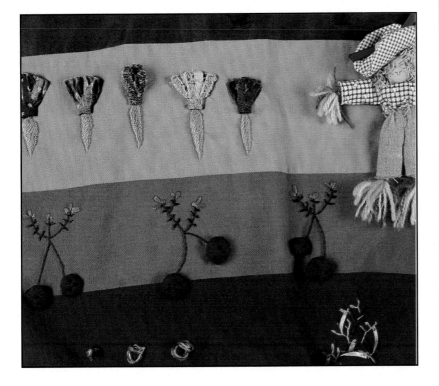

STEM STITCH

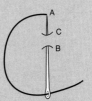

1. Come up at A, holding thread to left.
Go down at B and up at C. Pull through.

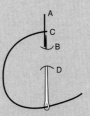

2. Go down at D, holding thread to the left.
Come up at B (DB equals CB). Pull through.

OUTLINE STITCH

The outline stitch is made by following
the above directions but holding the thread
to the right of the needle instead.
This stitch will furnish a straighter line.

■ Lettering ■

Background requirement – lightweight, medium weight, or stabilized fabric.

Attention to detail, as far as I'm concerned, is what embellishing is all about! Numbers and letters can direct attention to a particular area, identify a subject, make a statement, or even be part of the design. They can be sewn with consistency in a variety of sizes and styles, using one of the many computerized sewing machines that offer these pre-programmed stitches. If you don't have access to this technology, try dropping the feed dogs on your machine and sew free-motion words or numbers. Naturally this does require practice!

Hand embroidery is another technique that works well to create letters and numbers, except when a very small size is desired. A fine line permanent pen is a good alternative. Fabric pens make tracing letters or numerical stencils onto fabric simple to do. (Be sure they say permanent.) Quilters are using a variety of these methods to document their quilts with labels stating a host of information. Use the following advice to assist you when adding lettering to your work:

1. Be sure to stabilize the fabric if necessary, especially for machine lettering.

2. It will be easier to write on fabric if freezer paper has been pressed to the wrong side.

3. Always test, using a scrap of fabric from your project. Check thread color, tension, stabilizer, and most important, stitch and size. Now is the time to make adjustments.

4. Rather than cutting fabric to size and attempting to center the lettering in that space, use a generous piece of fabric and do the lettering first. Once the lettering is in place, simply cut out the correct unfinished size and proceed to piece or appliqué it in place.

RIGHT: A DAY AT THE BEACH WITH THE GIRLS, detail. The lettering on the 4½" x 2" sign for the Bovine Bar & Grill was done with the aid of my Pfaff® sewing machine. (Full view, page 81; detail, page 76).

PHOTO: RICHARD WALKER

■ Specialty Threads and Materials ■

Background requirement – any lightweight, medium weight, or stabilized fabric
(machine embroidery usually requires some form of stabilizing).

Run, don't walk to the nearest full service quilt, fabric, needlework, or yarn shop for specialty threads and materials. Don't overlook sewing centers or craft stores. Specialty products are available on spools, on tubes, and in skeins – the variety will amaze you. You'll discover a wide range of materials that can be applied by hand or machine for surface designing. I hesitate to provide a list for fear it will limit you to those mentioned, but to push you in the right direction, here are some that have been helpful to me: Sulky® rayon thread – solid and variegated (30 and 40 weight), Sulky® metallic thread, and Maderia®, Decor®, and Krienek® products. Generic merchandise like pearl cotton, decorative serger threads, ribbon and silk ribbon floss, crochet and tatting yarns, and knitting and weaving yarns are other possibilities to explore.

If you've experienced difficulties machine sewing with these threads, try replacing your regular sewing machine needle with a top-stitching Metalfil® or Schmetz® embroidery needle which has a larger eye. This will help prevent the problem of fraying and breaking, a common complaint with specialty threads. If the eye of the needle can't accommodate the size of the thread, try winding it on the bobbin by hand and sew with the wrong side facing you – this is called bobbin drawing. I'm repeating myself, but test, test, test before working on your masterpiece – and stitch slowly!

Traditional hand sewing techniques such as embroidery and couching work well too. Couching is a method of attaching a narrow cord, ribbon, or even decorative yarn to fabric by stitching it in place. Always select thread that closely matches the material being couched. Sew by taking diagonal stitches: come up and go down in the fabric next to the very edge of whatever you are couching.

If you are a machine person, use a zigzag stitch adjusted so the needle falls just off the edge, on either side of your couching material. Clear nylon thread works well for machine applications but I avoid it for handwork.

Computerized sewing machines featuring a vast selection of programmed embroidery stitches have certainly expanded my embellishing options. Gold color Sulky® rayon thread and some experimenting yielded the effective cross stitch trim on the playing cards featured on the jacket QUEEN OF HEARTS. Don't dismay if these options aren't available on your machine, as long as it's equipped with a zigzag stitch, you'll be able to add interesting details to your pieces. Try the following directions to stitch your own creations.

1. Draw a design on paper to fit the area you wish to embellish. Quilting motif pattern books are a good place to look for designs to trace.

2. Transfer the design to the right side of the fashion fabric. A light box is helpful here.

3. Set your machine for a narrow zigzag stitch. Use the proper needle for the type of thread you've chosen. Test stitch on a scrap of fabric from your project, using whatever stabilizing method you prefer. Now is the time to make adjustments, not after you've sewn on your masterpiece!

4. Stitch the design, remove stabilizer if necessary, and admire!

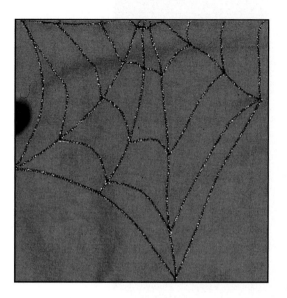

TRUE CONFESSION

Using the method just described, I created a spider web using variegated silver and black metallic thread. It looked terrific on my sample and all the while I was machine stitching it on my garment. When I had the chance to view the design from a distance it got an "F." It barely showed – I had invested all my time and effort, and it just disappeared! Moaning loudly, I went back to my test sample and played some more. I finally got the results I needed by stitching over the design a second time using black metallic thread! The moral of this story is be sure to view the test samples at a distance as well as close up.

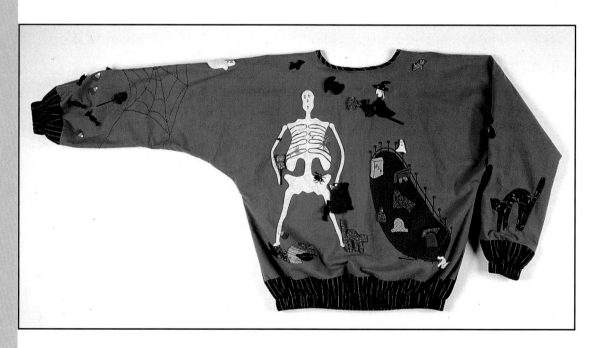

New ideas are generated with every project. Yarn snips become haystacks and braided pearl cotton is transformed into angel's hair. My folk art style forgives a great deal, but not baldness! Experience and practice in using these specialty items will expand your embellishment options.

LEFT, TOP: **BOO!**, detail. A simple zigzag stitch created the spider web on this pullover shirt. (Front view, page 35; back view, page 70; detail, page 34.)
PHOTO: RICHARD WALKER

LEFT, BOTTOM: **BOO!**, back view. (Front view, page 35; details, page 34, 70, 83.)
PHOTO: RICHARD WALKER

RIGHT, TOP: **ARE THE STREETS IN HEAVEN REALLY PAVED WITH FABRIC?**, detail. Braided pearl cotton created a fashionable hairstyle for this angel. (Front view, page 43; back view, page 61; details, page 61, 78.)
PHOTO: courtesy of QUILTER'S NEWSLETTER MAGAZINE

RIGHT, BOTTOM: **PEAKY & SPIKE – DOWN ON THE FARM**, detail. Collection of Doreen Speckmann. Ordinary yarn was snipped into small pieces and glued onto a triangle of muslin fabric. When completely dry, I appliquéd the muslin to the garment and added the 3-D detail. (Front view, page 45; detail, page 58.)
PHOTO: MARY STORI

■ Ribbon, Trim, Cording, & Piping ■

Background requirement – medium weight or stabilized fabric.

This section addresses embellishing materials that are wider or thicker than the ones discussed in the previous section. Ribbon and trim can be found in numerous widths and oodles of styles such as: grosgrain, satin, brocade, woven, braided, printed with designs, and decorated with glitter, rhinestones, and studs. Look for metallic covered cordings, which are manufactured in a wide variety of diameters and are twisted or braided. I also utilize soutache braid and rattail braid for decorative touches in quilts and garments. Plain cotton cording materials are useful when making your own piping or ruched cording.

I depend on ribbons and trims to help the eye distinguish and separate objects. For instance, the contrast of a piece of ribbon or narrow cord utilized to create a small flagpole may make it more visible than it would be if you were using its fabric counterpart. It would also be easier to apply the shape using trim than to piece or appliqué such a very tiny piece of fabric. With trim, the only finishing to be concerned with is each end. The top end can be hidden behind a flag, and the other end can be hidden behind grass or flowers at the base. If covering the ends is not possible, seam sealant will effectively deter fraying. Just

RIGHT: **YARD ART MEMORIAL PARK, full view, 49" x 40", 1993. The flagpole doesn't get lost on this quilt thanks to the shiny piece of cord that helps to keep it visible in spite of its size. (Details, page 29, 74, 88.)**

PHOTO: RICHARD WALKER

about any method of hand or machine stitching can be used to add any of these materials to a project. I prefer to use thread whenever feasible, but fabric glues work well too.

Fancy trims are fun to incorporate in both garments and quilts. Black braided trim was hand stitched to the background to simulate an iron entry arch to the Yard Art Memorial Park in my quilt of the same title. Gold braid was hand couched with gold metallic thread in my coat QUEEN OF HEARTS (see detail page 69). In KODAK MOOoooMENTS, made for the 1993-94 Fairfield Fashion Show with fabrics hand dyed by Lunn Fabrics, silver braid was hand couched with silver metallic thread (see page 75).

Sometimes I also add cording to my garments, to unify the design. To arrange a continuous line of cording that wanders around a garment, the cording is applied after the piece is constructed, but before it's lined. My preference for stitching method is hand couching, which allows me to maintain better control in directing the cording's placement.

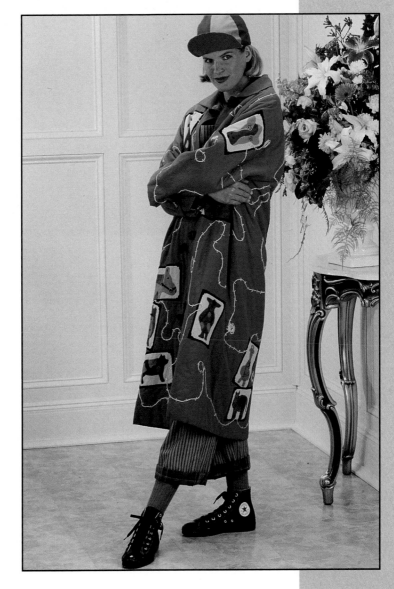

RIGHT: **KODAK MOOoooMENTS**, front view, 1993. Made for the 1993-94 Fairfield Fashion Show. (Details, page 83, 87.)
PHOTO: courtesy of FAIRFIELD PROCESSING CORP.

LEFT: **YARD ART MEMORIAL PARK**, detail. The specialty trim I found in a craft store was exactly what I'd been searching for to create the iron arch. (Full view, page 73; details, page 29, 88.)
PHOTO: RICHARD WALKER

■ Lace ■

Background requirement – lightweight, medium weight, or stabilized fabric.

It's difficult to refrain from writing a dozen paragraphs pertaining to each of the embellishing options in this chapter. The possibilities lace offers are no exception to the temptation! As many do, I've classified lace as anything that is white or ecru, has open-work, and is frilly. It could be long, narrow, and ribbon-like; wide and gathered; or even doily-like; and I'd still lump it into the one category called "lace." Technically this isn't correct, but for the purpose of this discussion "lace" will refer to all types including tatted, crocheted, woven, bobbin, and even those that are laser stamped on huge commercial machines.

I've used beautiful antique lace pieces to fully adorn garments, smaller pieces to trim a cuff or collar, and very small pieces to make petticoats or swimsuits for whimsical characters on a quilt. Look for lace at garage sales, flea markets, vendor's booths at quilt shows, fabric and craft stores, import shops, and anywhere bridal fabrics are sold. In addition to its beauty, working with lace offers several advantages. It's lightweight, is flexible, and is easily added by hand or machine. When lace trims are cut apart you'll need to finish the ends by hemming them, using a seam sealant, or hiding them in a seam.

LEFT: **A DAY AT THE BEACH WITH THE GIRLS,**
detail. A small piece of lace was easily manipulated
and hand stitched in place to provide a stylish
beach dress for this 2¼" 3-D Holstein cow. (Full
view, page 81; detail page 67.)

PHOTO: RICHARD WALKER

BELOW: **MARY, MARY, HOW DOES YOUR GAR-
DEN GROW? WHY WITH FABRIC, OF
COURSE!** #1, detail of garment back. A single tatted glove given to me by a friend made this bouquet of flowers special! It was further embellished
with a ribbon bow and half of an inexpensive ring
from a craft store. (Back view, page 39.)

PHOTO: RICHARD WALKER

■ Specialty Fabric ■

Background requirement – any fabric.

There are times when I've failed to locate the perfect fabric after hauling out stacks to consider. The explanation is simple – my shelves are full of 100% cottons and at times they just won't do! Once I finally drag out my containers of specialty fabrics, success is usually not far off. Small amounts of Ultra-Suede® upholstery and drapery fabrics, satins, sheers, and lamés go a long way in my folk art style. Since limited amounts are used, it's not necessary to get terribly concerned about the effect the uneven weight will have.

I've used gray satin to suggest a mirror, yellow ribbing for socks, and netting for tutu's. A scrap of silver lamé made a perfect thimble.

LEFT: **ARE THE STREETS IN HEAVEN REALLY PAVED WITH FABRIC?**, detail. What would heaven be like without a thimble? Thanks to silver lamé this angel won't have to find out! (Front view, page 43; back view, page 61; details, page 61, 71.)
PHOTO: courtesy of QUILTER'S NEWSLETTER MAGAZINE

RIGHT, TOP: **DELLA'S DANCE COMPANY,** front view, 1990. Specialty fabrics help to convey the feeling of dancers on stage. Notice lace is used to help create the costumes as well.
PHOTO: JIM ALEXANDER NEWBERRY

RIGHT, BOTTOM: **DELLA'S DANCE COMPANY,** back view. Netting, ribbing, lace, satin, and silk all contribute to this backstage scene.
PHOTO: JIM ALEXANDER NEWBERRY

79

■ Paints ■

Background requirement – any lightweight, medium weight, or stabilized fabric.

If you are unfamiliar with fabric paints, walk into any large craft store or fabric chain store that carries craft supplies, gaze down the aisle of paint products and be prepared for a shock! Yes, I said aisle – new merchandise hits the shelves regularly. I'm not referring to fabric dyes. My experience there is limited to tan Rit® dye, which I prefer over tea dyeing. Specialty paints are available in slender pen form and chunky markers. They can also be applied using a paint brush, airbrush, rollers, stencils, sponges, or stamps. Squeeze bottles fitted with special tips which are designed to dispense free-flowing lines for writing or drawing are another option. Need I say it – experiment! You'll find paints that puff, shine, glitter, and glow with iridescence. Please take the trouble to read the label when shopping. You want permanent fabric paint, which often means setting the paint with the heat of your iron. Some paints are not recom-

mended for items that need to be laundered. Analyzing your goal is the best way to find the proper tool to use; testing and practicing will confirm your selection.

Though this method of adding design through paints is one I use sparingly on my work, at least one of my quilts wouldn't be the same without it. A DAY AT THE BEACH WITH THE GIRLS was made for the annual Silver Dollar City Invitational Wall Quilt Challenge. The rules required the quiltmaker to create a 36" square quilt using selected fabrics provided by one of the sponsors, SPRINGS®. No substitutions were allowed. The Holstein "girls" would certainly look bare without their black spots and the shark in the ocean would only be another pale white fish without the gray glitter paint. Painting was a simple solution that enhanced these stuffed 3-D shapes!

81

Clear glitter paint highlights the tornado in the quilt TORNADO OF MEMORIES IN CHRIS'S CLOSET. This secondary embellishing application was not planned. The gray and black striped fabric worked well for the whirlwind until the patches with their white backgrounds were added. The white took over, visually merging the tornado into the background. Once painted, subtle light reflections off the glitter helped the tornado to become distinguishable from the background.

One of the hottest new methods for surface design is stamping. Pelle's See-Thru Stamps™ were used to create the milk bottles and cow images seen on the coat lining (100% cotton, hand-dyed Lunn Fabrics) of KODAK MOOoooMENTS. An inked stamp pad, a few custom-made stamps, and a little testing were all the tools I needed to add this humorous "icing on the cake" to my 1993-94 Fairfield Fashion Show Garment.

LEFT: **TORNADO OF MEMORIES IN CHRIS'S CLOSET**, detail. Clear glitter paint helps to prevent the tornado from fading into the background. (Full view, page 85; detail, page 94.)

PHOTO: RICHARD WALKER

BELOW, LEFT: **KODAK MOOoooMENTS**, detail of coat lining. Custom made stamps by Pelle's See-Thru Stamps™. I stamped the milk bottle onto the fabric and hand painted the "milk." When dry, I stamped the word "milk" for that final touch. (Front view, page 74; detail, page 87.)

PHOTO: courtesy of FAIRFIELD PROCESSING CORP.

BELOW, RIGHT: **BOO!**, detail. Black paint helped create this skeleton. (Front view, page 35; back view, page 70; details, page 34, 70.)

PHOTO: RICHARD WALKER

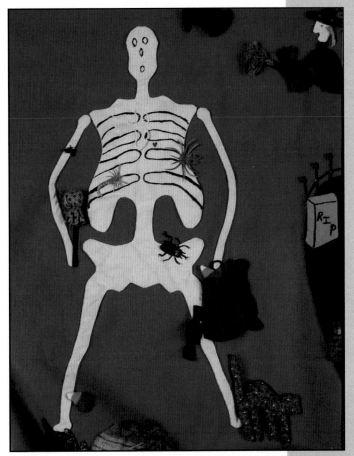

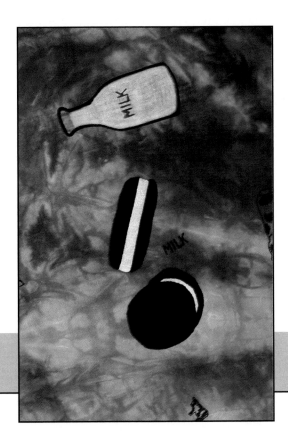

■ Patches ■

Background requirement – lightweight, medium weight, or stabilized fabric. (Do not fuse if batting is used as a stabilizer.)

A 1989 Youth Soccer – Division Championship patch or an Illinois Scholastic Merit emblem may not motivate you, but they certainly inspired my creativity! I've since concluded I may have been motivated by the sheer number of patches. I couldn't bear to toss out all those memories. If you find yourself in possession of a collection – or there is the remotest chance you might be encouraged to start one – read on.

Naturally patches and emblems can be machine or hand stitched in place but you may wish to consider the new approach I used to attach patches to a quilt top. Fusing this type of material is not a new idea. But after contemplating the time required to make a template for each shape, cut it from fusible webbing, and then fuse the patch (hoping I had measured correctly so the melted web didn't get all over my iron) I didn't find the prospect very appealing. Instead, I decided to use a liquid fusible product called Fusi-Tac® by Beacon. This glue is applied in liquid form, right from the plastic bottle to the wrong side of the patch. The patch is then fused in place. The results were very satisfactory, but please be sure to read and follow the manufacturer's directions.

■ Beads ■

Background requirement – any lightweight, medium weight, or stabilized fabric. (Use lightweight backgrounds with caution.)

I truly love working with beads. Some sparkle and shine just like twinkling lights on a Christmas tree, while others cast a subtle glow. That's only the beginning of the contribution beads can make. I'm reminded of the famous potato chip slogan (with a slight variation) – "No one can use just one!" Since volumes have been written on this wonderful embellishment technique, it's hard to pinpoint the most helpful information to share. I've narrowed my recommendations to four:

•Purchase and use the best beads possible. I'm not telling you to go out and buy the most expensive beads you can find, but it's a good habit to check for quality, no matter what the price is. Lesser quality beads, especially lesser quality bugle beads, can have sharp and uneven edges. These edges can cause the thread to wear, even break, and may also damage fabrics. Beading is time consuming – don't waste your time by using inferior products.

•Use beading thread such as Belding Corticelli's Nymo® or Nifty Notions Beading Thread®. These nylon threads won't stretch or break like sewing thread and they help to eliminate the problem of sagging and loose beads. Place a tiny drop of seam sealant on every knot, for insurance.

•I apply beads using a backstitch to make them more secure.

•To obtain uniform fabric tension, bead in a hoop if possible.

RIGHT, TOP: **KODAK MOOoooMENTS**, detail, 1993. Silver bugle beads stitched at an angle next to silver cording present the viewer with the picture of a barbed wire fence. (Front view, page 75; detail, page 83.)

PHOTO: courtesy of FAIRFIELD PROCESSING CORP.

RIGHT, BOTTOM: **TIC-TAC COLOR BLOC**, detail, 1991. Beads were the perfect embellishment to create the geometric designs while adding subtle sparkle to an otherwise plain jacket. (Front view, page 46).

PHOTO: RICHARD WALKER

HINTS FOR INCLUDING BEADS

There are countless ways to add beads to both quilts and garments. Here's a short list of the roles they have played for me.

- A large red bead was painted with black stripes and acted like a beach ball.
- One medium size white bead became a volleyball, with the aid of a few lines drawn with a black permanent pen.
- Yellow glass seed beads cascading from the hand of a farmer's wife represented chicken feed for the hungry chickens at her feet.
- White oblong wood beads looked like eggs when they were sewn into the opening of a fabric basket.
- Blue glass beads made great waves.
- A shower of multicolored beads accentuated lightning bolts.
- The gates of heaven were beaded with pearls.
- Tiny seed beads worked well as eyes.
- Long slender wooden beads helped to create a bamboo fishing pole.
- Beads become a game of Tic-Tac-Toe.
- Silver bugle beads created a barbed wire fence when placed next to silver cording.
- Tiny clear beads resembled dew on flowers.
- Yellow opaque beads were stitched in the shape of an ear of corn and green ribbon floss added to the illusion.

■ Buttons, Charms, Trinkets, Pins, Costume Jewelry ■

Background requirement – medium weight or stabilized fabric.

I've combined these into one category since attaching most of these embellishments usually requires a needle and a good strong thread. (Your ingenuity will determine how you use these tools.) Thread which matches the color of the do-dads being attached is usually a safe choice, although bright red thread holding a yellow button to a purple garment could be a fashion statement! Be sure to securely sew metal charms and trinkets. If the metal is rough and sharp it can cut the threads; I often use quilting thread for these items. The biggest factor to keep in mind is weight. Some trinkets may be light as a feather, others extremely heavy. Buttons, charms, and trinkets can be found in unlimited shapes

LEFT: **YARD ART MEMORIAL PARK**, detail. The butterflies are costume jewelry pieces which have been given a second life! (Full view, page 73; details, page 29, 74.)

PHOTO: RICHARD WALKER

RIGHT: **RED SKY AT NIGHT**, front view, 1993. A costume jewelry star pin, purchased for $1.00 at a garage sale was the inspiration for this machine quilted vest. It's embellished with additional inexpensive pins, charms, and beads.

PHOTO: MARY STORI

and sizes for your decorating pleasure.

The design and construction method of your project will determine the best time to add these embellishments. For instance, if you've chosen to add dozens of tiny gold star charms so they twinkle brightly on a quilted jacket, I'd recommend adding them after the quilting and construction process. Imagine what a headache it would be to have all those dangling objects snagging the fabric as you quilted.

Don't overlook the possibilities costume jewelry presents. Garage sales and flea markets are good sources of inexpensive junk jewelry. When you've paid only fifty cents for a piece, you can risk taking pliers to a

necklace to remove that butterfly that would look much better on your quilt. Pins are plentiful and it might seem obvious how to attach them. However, I take one extra precaution to secure pins that fasten on the right side of the garment. A drop of hot glue placed on the closed fitting will keep it from opening accidentally. For a less messy procedure, place a small amount of hot glue onto a piece of scrap paper and quickly dip the tip of a pin into the glue and transfer the glue to the closed clasp, taking care not to get glue on the fabric. Any glue formulated to work on metal can be substituted, but may require a longer drying period.

■ Miniatures ■

Background requirement – stabilized fabric.

Miniatures can be a novel approach to embellishing, but not without special problems. I like the challenge of beading an ear of corn rather than purchasing a miniature, but creating an item myself is not always possible. The alternative is to hunt down a miniature that will work. My search for such embellishments includes a variety of sources such as craft, novelty, party, and decorating shops, and stores that cater to those building and furnishing dollhouses. Locating the subject needed isn't usually a problem, but finding the correct color and size often is. The other biggest obstacle is attaching the miniature to the fabric. My first choice is always to stitch the item in place – forget the machine here! Before you begin stitching the item to your piece, study the impact of the weight and bulk being added. Miniatures tend to be one of the few exceptions to my rule of embellishing before garment construction or quilting a quilt.

How do you know when to add such embellishments? Think things through. If the piece demands a lot of handling during the construction process and it's possible to add the embellishment later, do so. When stitching miniatures to the fabric is not possible, I resort to glue. Use a permanent, fast setting glue. I've had good luck with Beacon's Fabri-Tac® and Gem-Tac®, although there are many others available.

RIGHT, TOP: **BUT, DOCTOR!**, detail. Both the sewing machine and the small basket were purchased in the miniature department of a craft store. Each was added by stitching through all three layers of the quilt using quilting thread. (Full view, page 23).
PHOTO: RICHARD WALKER

RIGHT, BOTTOM: **PULLED FROM EVERY DIRECTION**, detail. Small, lightweight miniatures can easily be hand stitched to a project. Avoid sharp objects; they could cut a hole. Since the metal on the wooden hanger is bent over, there's little chance it will cause any damage. (Full view, page 25, 39).
PHOTO: RICHARD WALKER

■ Oddities ■

Background requirement – stabilized fabric.

Many unusual objects have found their way onto my garments and quilts as embellishments. Believe me, some of them had me muttering and stamping my feet in frustration as I fretted over how to attach the "stuff." Eventually a solution was found, leaving me smirking all day long! Here are a few examples:

• Antique obe sash – Looking at the embellished fan handle in TAKARA, I'm sure you wonder what made this so difficult. The nearly completed petit point embroidered design had been worked on a stiff netting in preparation for construction into an obe sash. After considerable thought and consultation with my fellow stitchers on this project, I finally took scissors in hand and cut the embroidered strip from the webbing, getting as close to the threads as possible without cutting them. The strip was basted in position and carefully hand sewn to the quilt. A line of soutache braid was stitched around the very edge to hide the tiny bit of netting still visible. The ends of the trim were butted where they met and covered with a painted paper bead.

• Artificial flowers – Several bunches of silk flowers adorn the hair of the Japanese figure in TAKARA. Flowers were trimmed about an inch down the paper coated wire stems, and florist tape was wrapped around the base of the bouquet to create one stem. This was gently maneuvered into an opening left in the appliqué area of the hair. The opening was stitched closed and the stem tacked in place. Since the flowers cascade downward, no stitching remains visible.

• Metal light bulb base – Believe it or not, a squashed light bulb base found in a parking lot was the perfect embellishment for one quilt project. What a coincidence, finding an object to fit a light bulb I'd designed only days before! The lamé base previously planned had to be replaced by this find, but how was this new embellishment going to be attached? A hammer and nail solved the problem. I drove the point of a nail into the metal making a hole in each corner. Since it would have been a hassle having to deal with the weight of this embellishment and the accompanying metal chain, I sewed them on after most of the quilting was completed. The area adjacent to the light bulb was left unquilted, making it possible for me to get my hand between the backing and batting to sew these final embellishments in place. The batting helped stabilize the added weight and anchored the many stitches required to sew these pieces in place so they were not visible on the backing.

• Plastic bugs – Tacky ten-cent bugs were another unplanned embellishment that turned out to be great fun! (See photo of BOO! page 83.) My original intention was to embroider worms crawling through the skeleton. I instantly changed my mind when these creatures caught my attention while browsing through a craft store's Halloween display. A few posed no trouble to hand sew to the garment, but others were impossible. The glues I tested weren't satisfactory, which led to another idea. By heating the point of a pin in the flame of my gas stove, I was able to melt a hole in the plastic, allowing the bug to be treated like a button. Some serious grinning took place that day!

LEFT: **TORNADO OF MEMORIES IN CHRIS'S CLOSET**, detail. (Full view on page 85; detail, page 82.)

PHOTO: RICHARD WALKER

RIGHT: **MARY STORI**

PHOTO: JIM ALEXANDER NEWBERRY

THE FINAL TOUCH

There's much more for you to discover! Use this book as a reference to gather inspiration and information to enhance your projects with embellishments, bringing originality and uniqueness to your work.

Let me be your cheerleader in the game of embellishing. Go...Fight...Win! Be a good sport and remember to share your work with others!

～American Quilter's Society～

dedicated to publishing books for today's quilters